Reflections

Reflections

Seeking Serenity

Poetry by
CHAR FORSLUND

and Photography by
BRUCE ROWLAND

with Forewords by
KEN MORSE and STEVE ELDE

RESOURCE *Publications* • Eugene, Oregon

REFLECTIONS
Seeking Serenity

Copyright © 2025 Char Forslund. All rights reserved. Except for brief quotations in critical publications or reviews, no part of this book may be reproduced in any manner without prior written permission from the publisher. Write: Permissions, Wipf and Stock Publishers, 199 W. 8th Ave., Suite 3, Eugene, OR 97401.

Resource Publications
An Imprint of Wipf and Stock Publishers
199 W. 8th Ave., Suite 3
Eugene, OR 97401

www.wipfandstock.com

PAPERBACK ISBN: 979-8-3852-4177-4
HARDCOVER ISBN: 979-8-3852-4178-1
EBOOK ISBN: 979-8-3852-4179-8

Thank You

From Bruce:
Gustav Rowland
Ralph Varde
Steve Elde

From Char:
JaLynne Forslund
Lynn Baird
Ken Morse
and
John Nilson

Foreword

Poets grace us with words to help us embrace what is, cherish what was, and aspire to what might be. This requires the poet to be someone who has experienced life as it is and to marry this to the gift of well-chosen words to elicit a thought or feeling. This Char Forslund has done in this volume. It is the happy union of life and faith observed and polished like tumbling rocks over the course of a lifetime.

I learned early in our acquaintance that she had the charism of verse and saw this gift demonstrated when we taught together at the community where she resides. Her choices with words, with cadence, with focus make her work a place to return again and again.

Bruce's photographs are a wonderful counterpoint to Char's verse. Together they are thoughtful and life giving, hopeful and sustaining and suggest they have known each other for decades which they have.

May this book offer you the gift of hope retrieved, joy sustained and faith embraced again or for the first time.

Chaplain Ken Morse

Foreword

Bruce Rowland has been taking pictures for seven decades. Bruce sees the extraordinary in the ordinary and then frames it for the rest of us. His use of light, shadow, and color is like that of a master painter. Those things that we might walk past and miss completely, Bruce captures. Seeing his pictures makes us want to go back and find what we missed, to look for the hidden beauty in our lives. Bruce is an artist with lens and shutter. His images stir the depths. The pairing of his photographs with these poems brings together the power of words and image.

Steve Elde

New Every Morning

Eyes up!
Hearts up!
Minds sharp!
Compassion
on full blast!
Okay!
Let's go!
Good morning God!
We stand
under Grace,
ready to launch
Your new day!

Purple Praise

Trillium
explode your
purple majesty
on stalks of emerald
in the sunbathed yard.
Glory
crowned in velvet!
Praise heard today
and echoing throughout
eternity.

Whispers

Clamoring pounds
on the door of my being.
Onslaughts of the daily dredge
of all life's doings.
So, I withdraw within, with You,
to hush and still myself.
Seeking only quietude, gratitude,
and the wonder of simple things -
      a drifting leaf
        that soft bird call
          this breath I'm breathing
It is then I hear God
gently whispering
His Love and Grace.

Today's Walk

Sparse and spare,
relentlessly meager.
The hours of my day
stack up,
one upon another,
balanced precariously,
tempting the whole to fall.

And then You come,
sorting, sifting,
lifting the hand to balance,
speaking the Word to affirm,
throwing the lifeline that
defeats defeat,
and
I am saved.

Premise

New
Life
In
Christ
Turns on the premise that
Faith
Is
A
Verb.

The Bridge

Walking
one day, the words
between us spoke
of willingness
to help
to carry
the burden
a bit of the way.
So,
you leaned
toward me,
and I to you,
and we walked
one day,
bridging the open space
by stretching
out ourselves
to one another.

Thank God

For gentle things
that soothe my soul each day!
    the gold black flash of a butterfly wing
    the watercolor show of myriad dahlias
    the feisty perch of my favorite hummer
    the swoosh of water as it meets the shore
    the quick pure laughter of a friend
Oh! Thank God for gentle things
that touch and heal my soul!

Sunset

He flings
orange sherbert
across the universe,
icing my sky with
splendor and joy!
I simply sit
in awestruck wonder
murmuring,
"Yes Lord!
Yes indeed!"

Still

I still miss you.
A song in church
That piece of Scripture shared and loved
The dear sweet presence of a friend
A book, a smell, a laugh, a tear
And all the years come rushing back to me.
I miss you.

Trio

Now abideth
    Faith,
    Hope,
    Love,
    these three.
God,
    grant that
    they abide
    in me.

RSVP

Jesus'
invitation
to the feast
is universal.
Attendance, however,
is limited
to those
who RSVP,
in the affirmative.

Sir Daffodil

Awakening early under
a blanket of golden sunlight,
he stretched his
fluted throat skyward
belting out,
    "This little light of mine,
      I'm gonna let it shine…."
And laughing in response,
every bud and blossom in the meadow
joined the raucous chorus.

Seasons

Today's Reminder:
Cherish
the barren branches
framing my window.
Your beloved Quaking Aspen
is wintering and restful,
filling up with hope for Spring
and the burst of new life.
God's promise to my friend the tree,
and to me.

Author! Author!

Christ
is the author
of the drama
and
the leading character.
I have been chosen
to be a player
in the play.
Provided
I present myself
daily
for each enactment.

Boxes

Lord,
I admit that a lot
of my theology
is built from
a posture of fear.
Please, grant me
enough of Your Grace
to tear apart the boxes
of my beliefs that limit You.
And set me free!

Chrysalis

God saw me one day,
sheltering
in the dark end
of my cocooned life.
Gently,
He drew
apart the threads
until I
squirmed about
to face Him.
"Open your eyes to the
Light, beautiful creature.
I made you for
freedom.
I want you to fly."

Delivered

Today
was definitely
a dead letter day.
Lord,
seal me
in an envelope
of Your love and
send me winging.
I want to be
delivered.

Just Past Dawn

A ventured peek outside
yields yet another winter sky.
Pressing heavy air,
dense, somber greys,
the unmistakable scent of snow.
My bulbs clasp hands
and shiver in their soil caves,
longing for Spring.

He Who Has Ears

Complacency
held captive in
the fence of my
free will,
eats all the grass,
gorging on the here and now,
oblivious
to the call of eternity.

Hope is
>	the gift from God
>	that allows
>	my wail in the darkness
>	from the nest

of my faith.

Joy is
    the instantly
    accessible
    assurance
    of the
    adequacy
of God.

Just Fishermen

On a rocky beach
on that bleak dawn
they gathered together,
sad, confused, bereft.
Returning to the known,
but immersed in the yet unknown.
Then He appeared,
    "Breakfast is served,
        Come and eat",
and all thought to be lost,
was found.

Portrait

My life draws a pencil sketch,
    images outlined, some filled in.
Each day's events,
    joys, sorrows, loves, losses,
all add lines to the
    intricacies of my portrait
    which, when complete,
I will offer as a gift to God,
    as He offered himself to me,
framed in love.

Invitation

Soft colored layers
from the Creator's paintbrush
coax me to the water's edge.
Scents of fresh, clean air invite me.
Come to the bench.
> Just sit.
> Be still.

Simply breathe the beauty,
and be renewed.

On the Porch

At day's end I often take a steaming cup outside,
    along with all the bumps and bruises
    of the day that seek to
    wound my soul and steal my joy.
There I watch You joyously end Your day
    by splashing the sky in shades
    and hues of celebration!
I sit and sip, snuggly wrapped in
    the healing gift of Your love,
    my Creator God

Pause

Just a simple prayer,
God.
Deepen my desire
to truly know
You.

Raspberry Sorbet Sky

Colors yet unnamed
flood my tiny horizon
of Your Creation.
I wonder if
You laugh out loud
as You paint my good morning sky
and watch my dawning smile.
Some just call it sunrise.

Reminder

When the focus gets blurred,
and who I am has fuzzy edges,
I look to You
to sharpen the view
and remind me who I truly am,
a chosen child,
Yours!

Rest Stop

Gentle me, Jesus,
    for the day
    is long,
    and stretched,
    and taut.
    I despair.
Quiet me, Jesus.
    Hold me
    next to the
    steadfast beating
    of Your heart
    of love.
Turn me, Jesus,
    back into
    this day.
Complete and
    whole in You,
    I am repaired.

Daisies

    sooner or later
    you do have to stop
    counting petals on daisies.
    He does love you!
    now what?